<u>Other Hay House Titles</u>
<u>by Loretta LaRoche</u>

All of the above are available at your local bookstore,
or may be ordered by visiting:

Hay House USA: **www.hayhouse.com**®
Hay House Australia: **www.hayhouse.com.au**
Hay House UK: **www.hayhouse.co.uk**
Hay House South Africa: **orders@psdprom.co.za**
Hay House India: **www.hayhouseindia.co.in**

Squeeze the DAY

365 Ways to Bring JOY and JUICE into Your Life

Loretta LaRoche

HAY HOUSE, INC.
Carlsbad, California
London • Sydney • Johannesburg
Vancouver • Hong Kong • Mumbai

Published and distributed in the United States by: Hay House, Inc.: www.
hayhouse.com • **Published and distributed in Australia by:** Hay House Australia
Pty. Ltd.: www.hayhouse.com.au • **Published and distributed in the United
Kingdom by:** Hay House UK, Ltd.: www.hayhouse.co.uk • **Published and distributed
in the Republic of South Africa by:** Hay House SA (Pty), Ltd.: orders@psdprom.co.za
• **Distributed in Canada by:** Raincoast: www.raincoast.com • **Published in India
by:** Hay House Publications (India) Pvt. Ltd.: www.hayhouseindia.co.in • **Distributed
in India by:** Media Star: booksdivision@mediastar.co.in

Editorial supervision: Jill Kramer • *Design:* Amy Gingery

Library of Congress Control Number: 2005937306

ISBN 13: 978-1-4019-0890-4 • **ISBN 10:** 1-4019-0890-X

09 08 07 06   4 3 2 1
1st printing, April 2006

Printed in the United States of America

*Every woman needs some great male
friends in her life, and I'm lucky enough
to have them in Gregg, Ken, and Scott.
To the many laughs we've had,
and the loving friendship we share. . . .*

Introduction

As a stress-management consultant over the last 20 years, I've seen the levels of stress and anxiety in people escalate to the point where it feels that everything including breathing is now stressful. It has become so much a part of the American culture that a huge industry of products and practitioners has emerged to handle the "stress epidemic." We even have experts who work on relieving stress in children and pets.

I appreciate that the traditional models of stress management can be helpful—things like meditation, exercise, and cognitive behavioral therapy. But it's equally, if not more, important to focus on filling our days with fun, fantasy, and fantastic thoughts that can lift our spirits and bring us joy. When we stop obsessing over what's wrong in our lives and instead pay attention to our strengths, talents, and the wonders around us, everyday stresses become much more manageable. As I always love to remind people: "If you think the worst and get the worst, you suffer twice; if you think the best and get the worst, you only suffer once."

In the course of my work, I've found that it's often the quick, funny thoughts that people can easily digest and remember that are the most helpful. So I've compiled this book of one (hopefully) memorable thought for every day of the year. Read through it with an open mind. You may laugh at some, delight in others, or be stimulated to change some of your irrational behaviors. (And believe me, I know it's hard to admit it, but we all have them, including me. How do you think I know so much about this stuff?) Most important, I hope that you'll enjoy reading this book as much as I did writing it!

— **Loretta LaRoche**

We live in a world of excess, in which how much we own defines who we are. I'd rather *be* "too much" than buy too much. It's so much easier. I'll never have to have a yard sale to get rid of myself. . . .

If life hands you lemons, you could become bitter, too—or you could make lemonade—but frankly, I'd rather just throw them out and get something I really want instead.

3

You could torture yourself with an

exhausting thousand-mile journey

of self-discovery . . . but why not take

a jet plane instead and have fun

sooner rather than later?

In order to be fully alive, you first
have to be awake and aware, otherwise
you're simply sleepwalking.

5

Be fully present with your friends, family, and co-workers. Nobody wants to talk to someone who's mentally practicing for the future while pretending to listen.

When your life begins to resemble

a B movie, change direction,

and think like a master filmmaker.

You just may win an Oscar.

7

Keep passion in your life. The
fire from it will keep your soul
from turning to ashes and your
mind from turning to mush.

8

If you're always trying to be

right about everything you do and

say, you'll soon find that you have

no one around you who's interested

in how right you are.

Challenge your brain in new and creative ways. It will help stop you from doing the same thing day after day like Bill Murray in *Groundhog Day*.

10

Put on some music and dance with wild abandon. It will free you to become more at ease with your body and all the wonderful movements it can make.

11

Try to make a difference in the life of

someone who's less fortunate than you,

because one day you may take their

place and they may take yours.

12

When your mind tries to become your

master, realize that you must use your

inner power to master your mind.

13

Every day be grateful for what

you're capable of instead of what

you can't or didn't do. It will

give you much more peace.

14

Know that if you allow others to be

themselves, then you can stop focusing

on trying to clone yourself.

15

Be grateful for "breakthroughs."

They can help keep you free from

breakdowns, burnouts, and all other

types of ups and downs.

16

There's nothing like enthusiasm.

It fills the air with bubbles of joy

just like the ones we loved as children,

streaming out of bottles filled with

magical, soapy water.

17

If you can laugh every day,

especially at yourself, you've

found the best joke in the world.

Many of us have analyzed our lives to the extent that we begin to display "analysis paralysis." Sometimes it's better to leave something unexamined. The problem might just go away on its own.

19

When you thank others for what
they've done on your behalf,
you're sending them a blessing
and the gift of respect.

Doesn't it seem as if instead of talking to one another, all we do is leave messages for one another to *avoid* talking? We're so attached to our home answering machines, cell-phone voice mail, and e-mail that nobody actually talks to each other. Why don't we just send ourselves messages and then delete them and get it over with?

21

Say what you mean and mean what you say. It allows you to be true to yourself, and you'll be less likely to feel guilty. And haven't we all had enough guilt? . . . the gift that keeps on giving.

22

Imagination is like a family. It can bring you fun, laughter, creative ideas, and helpful solutions. But it can also take you to places like hell and back. Make sure yours is working *for* you and not against you.

23

The world is filled with amazing
places to visit. Don't limit yourself to
the same destination all the time. Even
taking a different road home from the
office will broaden your horizons.

Try to remove the word *boring* from your vocabulary. You're actually admitting that you have very few assets to amuse yourself. Don't lose touch with your ability to access your inner muse.

25

Whenever you begin criticizing
yourself, stop and ask, "What's the
point?" If there is a point and you can
do something about it, do it. If you're
being self-critical over something ridiculous like the fact that you're "too short,"
then move on, and just think tall.

If we all ate less and moved more, the diet industry and the food police would go out of business, and we'd all have more money to just have fun.

27

Men and women are different! End of story. If you want your man or woman to behave like the opposite sex, then cut to the chase and live with your own kind.

Become playful instead of
grumpy when you're waiting in
line. It makes life so much easier,
and everyone profits from being
surrounded by lighthearted energy.
Ask the clerk to "check you out"
along with your bundles. She
may give you double coupons.

My mother always said, "You never know" as a kind of catchall anxiety producer. Whenever there was something she wanted us to do, it was because if we didn't, "You never know." I still don't know what I'm supposed to know, but that's okay because I'm finally not afraid to find out.

30

Make every day an adventure.
Become your own Lewis & Clark
expedition. When you stop seeking,
you become like an old fossil
waiting to be dug up.

Nature contains a wealth of wisdom.

And it's right outside your front door.

Don't mistake a treadmill for a walk in

the woods. Do both, but opt for woods

over a moving rubber sidewalk when-

ever you can. It will renew your spirit.

Eat a varied diet. Don't make one food the elixir of life. Salmon may be good for you, but you don't want to have to swim upstream and spawn.

If you wait for special occasions
to celebrate, you're not honoring
today. Why isn't today a special
occasion? You're still alive!

Try to incorporate pets into your life. They're amusing, affectionate, and their love is unconditional. If you have allergies, buy fish. Just watching them swim will help you from sinking into a bad mood.

35

Become available to irreverence.

When you begin to laugh at what you

hold sacred and *still* hold it sacred, you

have truly become an enlightened being.

When you go to sleep at night
and find your mind racing, sign
off by telling your inner self,
"I'll think about whatever you're
telling me tomorrow." It will be
tricked into leaving you alone.

Surround yourself with inquisitive, curious, intelligent, loving, kind, and funny people. (Yes, you can find them!) They'll keep your mood upbeat and your life focused on "generativity" versus stagnation.

Try to spend some time
every day being amused by the world
around you. There's more than enough
suffering to be aware of, but nothing
can refresh your spirits more than a
good laugh. It's like a cool glass
of lemonade on a hot day.

What would happen if we all spent
one day a week without complaining
about anything? Everything would
look better, feel better, and be less
irritating. Then we'd get along better,
and there'd be less to complain about.

When we take the time to be still
and meditate even for ten minutes a day,
we start to create more spaciousness
around our thoughts. And then we may
have the good fortune to have our fears
drift away to another galaxy while we
can keep the things we really need and
attach them to the luminous stars.

41

Remember that there's a
limit to how much baggage you may
carry on a plane, and the same rule
should apply throughout life. Get rid
of the suitcases filled with old anger
and resentment. You'll look better, feel
lighter, and you'll have much more
room in your suitcase. . . .

42

If you have children, allow them to see you as their parents. They already have friends. What they need are mature adults who set limits, teach values, and are responsible citizens of the world.

43

Keep in mind that nothing is written in stone but your tombstone. If you're flexible, you can change your mind, your plans, and the direction of your life. If you're not, you might as well live underground.

When you wake up in the morning,

shout out to the world,

"I'm back!" It acknowledges

the gift you've received to be

on this planet another day.

45

When you go to work, remember
that you applied for the job. You're
not a prisoner doing time. If you want
out, give yourself a parole: Seek work
that will make you feel free to be who
you are and allow you to do more
of what you want to do.

Don't use phrases like "You never help me" or "You never listen." They already know that—you've told them a hundred times. Use your energy to explain what you want, instead of what you're not getting.

47

Simply following the dictates of fashion
sometimes makes us look freakish, not
fashionable. The mirror often lies, especially when we don't want to accept the
truth. Use common sense and your inner
judgment about what looks good—
not what the magazines tell you is "in."

48

Belt out a song every once in a while

about the things that bother you. Take

your favorite sad tune and create lyrics

about some of the things that drive you

nuts. If you're going to feel blue, you

might as well *sing* the blues.

Eating is one of the greatest
joys in the world. Don't allow
yourself to "wolf your food down"
just so you can get to your next task.
That lack of awareness could result
in a stomach that will howl—
and perhaps a few added jowls.

50

Stay conscious of the fact that people around you can hear your cell-phone conversations. Find a private place, if possible, or speak more softly. Most of us don't really care that you closed the deal, finished your workout, got the kids to soccer practice, or finally made it to the grocery store. Enough already!

51

Try not to get hooked on your

computer, BlackBerry, or iPod.

It's like having an affair with a robot.

No flashy technology can take the

place of a great face-to-face conver-

sation with another human being.

52

Try doing something "old-world"
neighborly. Invite people over for
coffee. If someone's ill, bring them
some soup. Those sorts of simple acts
will create a community of support and
affection that enrich everyone involved.

53

If you're having a string of
failures, find a way to find the
"bless in the mess." Embedded
in the problems might be a way
to find future successes.

We're often told that our lives should be simpler, by "experts" whose ideas about paring down seem awfully complex and time-consuming. Wouldn't it be easier to learn to live with what we have or simply just stop buying more than we need?

55

The concept of learning how

to "live in the moment" is great,

but also be aware that planning for

tomorrow, next week, or next year

can bring you the excitement of

knowing that you might live

another couple of moments.

If your laughter quotient has
gone down significantly, you may be
spiraling into depression. Ask someone you can trust for some feedback.
Without a sense of humor, we're like
a fish fry without the grease:
dry, withered, and zestless.

Make sure your vocabulary gets a workout

periodically. We seem to be becoming a

nation with less and less interest in the beauty

and complexity of language. E-mails and con-

versations these days are beginning to sound

more Neanderthal. I think we're closer than

we think to a return to grunting . . . *ug!*

Wouldn't it be nice to have an answering machine that simply asked the caller, "Who are you, and what do you want?" That would really cut to the chase.

59

Don't turn yourself into a news nut.
It's fine to keep up with current
events, but when you obsess about
every bit of coverage, it can only
serve to create anxiety, distrust of
every living being, and fear about
everything from mold to mites.

60

Words such as *fine, okay, not bad,*
and *nice* can make you feel like you ate
but never got full. All of life deserves to be
explained in spicy, interesting, juicy terms.
How about *brilliant, remarkable, indescribable,*
and *profound?* Our lives often follow our
descriptions, so when you make your
words soar, you'll soon be flying.

61

When you're driving down the

road and you've missed your exit,

just be grateful it's not the final one.

62

Do you turn to TV or
other media simply as a way to
"waste time" rather than as a way
to enrich yourself? Do you really
believe you have so much time on
this earth that you need to find
ways to waste it?

If you're heavier than you'd like to be, pat the excess poundage tenderly and just acknowledge your part in the process. If you fed it, it's yours. It is what it is, so why create more struggle? When you're ready, you'll lose the weight. Until then, don't beat yourself up.

64

The next time you go
on a vacation, leave your laptop
computer, briefcase, and pager
at home. Or else, just have some
sand and a beach umbrella
delivered to your office.

65

Holding a grudge is like being

in an airplane that can never land.

It's exhausting, and it can wear out

your parts. Find an airport called

Forgiveness so you can get to your

final destination . . . *Happiness*.

Living a long, healthy life should be everyone's goal. But don't get too consumed with the facts, foods, and fancy exercises that are today's fashion for finding the fountain of youth. You might just get older faster from all the worrying about how to stay young.

When you're looking for a date on the Internet, make sure that you know that "trim, athletic, and attractive" seems to apply to everyone who breathes—regardless of how short, homely, and clumsy they might be. Remember—a picture is worth a thousand words. Especially one taken in this decade.

68

When you're alone and you

find yourself feeling lonely, think of

all the time you spent with people

who made you feel even *more* alone

while you were with them.

Try writing a note instead
of buying a "greeting card."
You know the other person;
the card company doesn't.

70

The flowers in your
garden can help you imagine
that the wisdom behind their
creation had to indeed be something
that knows what we humans would
find joyous and beautiful.

Riding a bike makes the wind rush by, the landscapes pop out, and your heart and lungs go "Whoopee!"

72

There's nothing like a cat
sitting at the end of your bed at
night. It makes you feel like you
have a feline bodyguard who
not only protects you, but loves
you unconditionally.

When you go to the market,

enjoy being able to buy the food and

share it with others. Yes, you have to put

it away, and yes, it will be gone soon, but

think about how fortunate you are to

be able to buy it and share it.

74

Spend more time being in
service to something greater than
yourself. Too much time spent on "me,
me, me" makes life feel like a planet
without the sun and the moon: dark
and lonely. Create a universal "we,"
which, in turn, will serve us all.

75

If you think the worst and get the worst, you suffer twice. If you think the best and get the worst, you only suffer once.

If you always think you have to go somewhere, then you're never really anywhere. Remember what Mother said: "You can't be in two places at once."

Don't waste energy trying to

change another person's behavior.

You'll get frustrated, they'll become

defensive, and no one wins.

When you sit down to dine, moan and groan with delight. Don't discuss what's in it that might give you heartburn; high cholesterol; or large, protruding pimples. It will only eat at you . . . while you're trying to eat.

79

Seek out someone who *cares* about you, not someone to *take care* of you. *You* are the only one who can take care of you.

When you go to bed at

night, count your blessings, not

your e-mails. It will give your mind

the message: "I have what I need.

Don't worry; all is well."

Try to be spontaneous, not robotic.

If you want a windup doll, go to a

toy store and buy one.

82

Taking a deep breath always

gives you the space to remove

yourself a bit from the rat race.

Just remember to *keep* breathing.

Make funny faces whenever

you can—especially in the morning

when you wake up. Why not start

your day as if you're a playful child

instead of a plodding horse.

Amazing things are possible

when you dwell in possibilities.

Can you stop focusing on the

things that keep you from living

out your dreams, and just

think about the dreams?

85

When you "grin and bear it,"

you feel isolated and alone. Develop

the ability to "grin and share it," and

you'll find a world filled with comfort,

compassion, and caring.

Choose one day a week to consciously do things differently. Brush your teeth with the opposite hand, dance around the house and sing to yourself or your family, and wear something that's totally outside the norm. You might find that you're more interesting than you thought you were.

87

Stop comparing yourself with others. Wishing you were more like someone else is like trying to turn a table into a chair. Just make the most of what you have.

88

Don't get stuck on the need
for everything to be fair. The fallacy
of fairness can leave us agitated,
and obsessed with wanting justice in
every situation. Right wrongs when
possible with grace and dignity.
And leave the rest to God.

Look in your closet on a regular basis to see if your clothes are starting to give birth to themselves. It may be a sign that you should "drop out of shopping" instead of "shopping till you drop."

90

If you've become a drama diva, you may want to stop driving your friends and family nuts and just go out and audition for a soap opera. At least that way you can get fan mail.

You've all heard the phrase
"Never say never." But sometimes you
really do need to say it—like if your
ex-husband or wife asks you to remarry
them. They didn't become an ex for
nothing. And sometimes you should
lock the door behind you.

When your kids say they're bored and need some entertainment, take them to a homeless shelter and have them volunteer their services. They may suddenly realize that their so-called boring lives would make some people feel like kings and queens.

93

When you come to the end of

your life, hopefully the memo-

ries your loved ones have of you

will be more valuable to them

than the reading of your will.

94

Take the time to write a list of all your

strengths. As for your weaknesses . . .

everyone's already familiar with those,

including you. Success is produced

by strength, not weakness.

95

If you're waiting for some-

one important to give you

"permission" to have fun . . .

forget it. They're not coming.

They're out having a good time.

Stress is not all bad. It can be

a positive source of energy.

It is dis-stress that we need to

be aware of and change.

Do you do dumb things when you're overstressed, such as yelling at your dog? If so, the next time you yell at Fido, can you recognize that *he* isn't the problem—you are. Sit down with the dog and share a biscuit.

Are you addicted to stress-relief products? There's nothing wrong with candles and the sound of running water, but don't kid yourself into thinking that's changing the problem. You might just find yourself urinating constantly, with the curtains on fire. And you'll still have your problems.

Now and then, get a massage. There's nothing like touch to soothe "skin hunger." Even if you think you won't like it, your body will!

100

Do you spend way too much time thinking about what you "should" have done? If so, stop "shoulding" on yourself!

101

Life's accomplishments can

only happen when you take risks.

However, make sure the risk is

appropriate to the situation.

102

Don't wait to have fun. Your chores will never be done—face it! Instead of putting off the fun, put off the tasks. They'll still be there waiting for you—you can be sure of that! Or, best of all, find a way to have fun *while* doing your tasks.

Life is in the little things. We all agonize over the details, such as "Why am I vacuuming? The rug will just get dirty again tomorrow!" We need to learn to appreciate that the little things are a part of any good life. You don't get to vacuum if you're homeless.

Just because the menu says that the chicken is "free range" and "young" doesn't mean that it is—or that it should cost ten times more than it does in a supermarket. Sometimes the ordinary is just as extraordinary as the exotic. A good hot dog on a bun with sauerkraut ain't bad.

105

A wet towel on the bed

or a glass of spilled milk is not a

crime. Stop catastrophizing—you'll

have more strength to handle a

real mugging, God forbid.

You're not getting

out of this life alive.

107

Put your hand on your heart

and think about people who have

brought you love and joy. You will

feel incredible peace.

108

There's nothing wrong with fidgeting.

Don't try to get your kids to sit still—

that's the wrong message to send them

about movement. Soon enough, they'll

be paying for a gym membership!

For now, let 'em work off the anxiety.

Don't delude yourself into thinking that hand-washed lettuce from the banks of the Euphrates River is any better for you than Bibb lettuce from the grocery store. And the former is $25 more a pound!

110

Give yourself a respite from noise. Now

and then, turn off the radio and the TV

and shut the windows. Your ears will

thank you, and your soul will flourish

from the sound of silence.

There's nothing like great sex to improve your mood. Find yourself someone delicious to share some desire with, or just have fun with yourself . . .

ooh la la. . . .

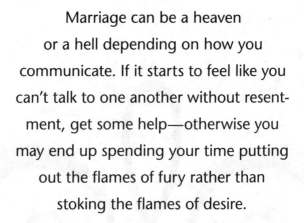

112

Marriage can be a heaven
or a hell depending on how you
communicate. If it starts to feel like you
can't talk to one another without resentment, get some help—otherwise you
may end up spending your time putting
out the flames of fury rather than
stoking the flames of desire.

Whenever you find yourself complaining about politics and how nothing good ever gets done, put pen to paper and make your complaints heard by those who may be able to act. Discussing your complaints with friends or family without some kind of action just creates more of the same . . . nothing.

114

Make sure you spend some
time creating a sense of community
for yourself and others—it's been
proven to extend life more than just
a healthy diet and exercise. Being
fit and alone is just not fun.

115

Don't give your children
everything they want. In the
long run, it won't be the way
to make them happy, and
they just might end up
never leaving home.

Isn't it time that every physician asked us, as part of a regular physical exam, if we're having any fun? What's the point of having low cholesterol, low blood pressure, and good blood sugar if you're a miserable wretch?

How necessary is it to worry about furniture placement? I know it's fun to feng shui your house, but don't get too nuts. Millions of people have survived over the years even though their mirrors were facing the wrong direction.

Whenever you can read a good book, it will expand your vocabulary, enrich your life, and give you the opportunity to meet new and interesting characters.

119

Don't become too wrapped up in
your children's after-school sports.
If you become obsessed with having
them win, to the point where it starts
to feel like a personal defeat when they
lose, it may be time for you to leave
them home and try out yourself.

120

Learn to use your anger in productive ways. It can be very healing as long as you don't use scare tactics, tantrums, and warlike methods that scare the neighborhood.

121

Try to spend time with an elder in your family to discover your history. Where did you come from, what were the rituals, who were the characters that came in and out, what were the favorite foods . . . ? There's nothing more exciting than becoming your own Smithsonian Institution.

122

Emily Post would turn over in her grave if she witnessed the rudeness that has become so much a part of the 21st century. Make sure that you and your family members respect each other and your fellow humans. It may save us from repeating the fall of the Roman Empire.

123

Don't you think we should all

stop sharing so much information?

Getting your teeth cleaned is a great

thing, but we don't need to know

what they found in the process.

124

Curiosity—
what a wonderful word.
Make sure you never lose your
need to discover new concepts, new
environments, or new people. It
helps keep you from becoming a
boring, repetitive individual.

125

Meaning in life is enhanced

when you discover a larger purpose

beyond yourself. It helps you avoid

the incessant "me, me, me," in

exchange for the global "we."

Sadness can be a process that helps take you through to gladness. If it lingers and seems to be leading to depression, seek help. But do not fear *some* darkness—it can often be the teacher that takes you to the light.

Have you ever found yourself in an argument that has no purpose other than to just be a forum for ranting? If you suddenly find yourself looking and sounding like a dog with a bone, you might want to take a time out to find something better to chew on.

This wonderful planet filled
with its spectacular array of plants,
animals, mountains, seas, and sky
is yours to admire and explore.
Honor and protect it as you would
your children so it can continue
to inspire those that follow.

Try not to make fun of other

people. Make your humor

inclusive, not exclusive.

130

I've never forgotten my grandmother Francesca's meatballs. Make sure you provide your family with foods that have a heritage. It makes your mouth feel happy and your heart sing.

Don't you just love walking on

the beach—the feeling of the sand

between your toes, and the way the

ocean knows how to come in and

out without a cell signal. . . .

I hate it when I'm talking to a
friend on the phone and she puts
me on hold for "call waiting." Shouldn't
the person who calls later be the one
who waits? Is call waiting really worth
it when it ruins the intimacy with
the person you're talking to?

Do you ever try browsing in small shops run by sole proprietors? It's so much better to find something unique that's made with love, rather than yet another piece of merchandise designed by a committee.

134

If you find yourself jumping
through hoops to find your children
the "hot" toy for the holiday, isn't this just
teaching them that happiness depends on
what marketers are hawking this season?
Wouldn't it be better to create an experience
that will give them memories, rather than a
toy that has nothing memorable to say?

Is a trip to an outlet mall really

the best way to spend one of your

precious days on Earth?

Do you really need any
more clothes, or are you shopping
for sport? Sometimes we all go a little
nuts and need to remember that it
might make some sense to shop in
our closets now and then. There's
some good stuff in there.

Don't you hate it when people you know tell you how busy they are when you ask them to get together? Because it often seems that what they're saying is that they're too busy to spend time with *you!* Sure, many of us have tough lives, but it's not too hard to find a way to squeeze in the people you like or love.

Try focusing your conversations

with others on the *extraordinary* as

well as the ordinary. It will keep

people interested and looking

forward to the next conversation.

Fake it till you make it! Every woman has learned that trick! Sometimes it really works to try smiling when you're down or acting silly when you're overwhelmed. The action might just turn around the emotion.

You have three options in any situation: Act upon it, avoid it, or accept it. Don't make it more complicated than that . . . choose one and move on.

141

Spend more time with children.

Watch how they avoid the serious

and head for the delirious. . . .

142

Remember that you are not the

center of the universe. It's much

more fun to *travel* the world than to

think that *you* are the world.

Why do something because
"they" said you should do it?
Don't live your entire life around
what "they" say is right for you.
Remember that you *are* them, so you
really should listen to yourself.

Strive for excellence, not perfection.

One is attainable and will make you feel

great; the other is impossible and will

make you feel inadequate.

145

Try to judge others less often.

You can't control them, and

you can't change them—

unless you're a plastic surgeon.

So live and let live.

Don't obsess about the weather.
How many times have you wasted
energy raging over the fact that it's
raining and you had plans? What
can you do? Treat yourself with
an indoor substitute—or act like
a kid and jump in the puddles!

147

Enjoy your solitude.

Nothing can be more refreshing

to the mind than some quiet time

for reflection, peace, and the freedom

to calmly enjoy the things that

you love most.

No whining! Don't you hate it when you hear kids do it? If you're so in need of whining, start a "global whining" group and do it with friends. You may start laughing instead.

Try to listen

as often as you talk.

You might learn

something new.

150

Stop suffering in advance.

Can you wait until

something bad really happens,

and then suffer—instead of

planning for it?

151

Get rid of the energy vampires.

If somebody drains the life out of you

whenever you talk to them . . . wear

garlic around your neck and move on.

152

If you spend a lot of time thinking

about all the things that are wrong

with you—try spending the same

amount of time thinking of the things

that are *right* with you. . . .

153

The next time you're feeling
"road rage," really try to remember
where you are. You're not in a coliseum
about to be attacked by lions. You're probably in a car equipped with "climate control,"
a stereo sound system, and a telephone.
Enjoy your luxurious surroundings and be
thankful for the traffic! Turn up the volume,
play air guitar, or call a friend!

154

When I was a kid and acted a little too "entitled," my mother used to say, "Just who do you think you are?" Even all these years later, when I finally know who I think I am, I wonder: *What the hell does that really mean? That I'd better understand how unimportant I really am?*

155

Instead of getting enraged, get

engaged! Engage your rational mind

and think: *What am I screaming*

about? Is it really all that important?

What's so cool about being "cool"? Statements like "Whatever" only make life feel like a dial tone, flat and uninteresting. Try to get excited more often. It's much easier to get a signal.

Be unique. If we all wear the same clothes from the same chain stores in the same malls, we might as well apply for the position of Stepford Wife. Wear something unusual, with your own flair.

I think a book called

I'm My Own Fault would be

one of the best self-help

books ever written.

Being "the best you
can be" is a great thing to
strive for, but don't forget
that you can be happy while
you're getting there.

160

Don't be afraid of eccentricity.
It's the eccentrics who make the
world an interesting, creative, and
unique place. Seek out the unusual,
in others and in yourself. Do you want
your tombstone to say: "He was a
lot like everybody else"?

161

Does anybody else really care about your
eating habits? How much fiber you've taken
in? How no fat ever passes across your lips?
Isn't that the most boring subject on Earth?
But people discuss it endlessly. Instead,
talk about how you're enjoying what you
can eat. People will connect with that!

162

In any painting, the dark colors can
be as beautiful as the light ones.
Don't think you always have to paint
a rosy picture. Sometimes sharing
the unpleasant things in life will make
you feel more real. . . .

163

How did you act out your
individuality as a child? Through
sports? Acting? Painting? Singing?
What turned you on then? Would it still
turn you on now? How can you bring
that kid back into your life?

164

If you thought about which is more important to you, family time or work time, you'd probably choose the former. But do you dare turn off your cell phone during vacations? Or even during dinner?

Do you really need a pager?
A BlackBerry? A cell phone?
A wireless PDA with Internet access?
Whatever level of portable communi-
cation device you have—do you really
need to be so in touch all the time?
Suppose someone had to wait a few
hours before they reached you?
Would anyone end up dead?

Do you laugh enough at work?
Unless you're running a trauma center,
there's got to be some room for humor
in your workplace. Laughter and joy
make you more creative and productive, so don't take your work so seriously and you'll probably do it better.

167

There's nothing

you should be doing "24/7"

except breathing.

168

You don't have to go somewhere special to get exercise. Instead of the escalator, take the stairs. Instead of the drive-through, park and get up off your butt. Adding extra steps to your life will help your heart, your lungs, and your attitude.

Don't kid yourself into believing that just because something is liquid, it's similar to drinking fresh, cool water. Frappuccinos and mocha lattes have as many calories as a 16-ounce rib eye.

Instead of a vitamin-C

supplement, how about eating

an orange?

Do you spend more time

dressing for the gym than exercising?

On days when you're feeling

"not quite right," allow your intuition

to guide you, and take some time to

be your own inner physician.

173

When you need some
companionship, do you turn to
television instead of friends or family?
Sure, TV is always available, but it never
talks back—and it leaves no lasting
memories—so what's the point?

174

Music enhances the functioning
of the brain: It can have calming
and stimulating effects, and some
studies have indicated that listening
to music has been proven to increase
creativity in children. Is music a
big enough part of your life?

175

Do you find yourself discussing reality shows with people instead of discussing your own reality? I bet it's a lot more interesting, and besides, *you're* the star!

The next time you buy a
$2 bottle of water, ask yourself:
*Why am I spending all this money for
something I can get for free? Is it really
any healthier than what comes out of the
tap, which is regulated by the local
water department?* Just because
it's called "Agua Nova" doesn't
make it safer or better.

Isn't the phrase "quality time" annoying? Is there *any* time that you spend with your family that should be second-rate time? Bargain-basement time?

After a national tragedy, people tend to be nicer to one another. Remember the days after September 11? Or for the baby boomers and older, after JFK was shot? Why does it take death, destruction, and fear for us to be pleasant to one another?

Share good news every day. And don't downplay it by adding something negative like "What a glorious day; enjoy it while it lasts because it's going to rain on Friday." Why dampen the joy? It doesn't serve any purpose other than validating some meteorologist's predictions.

180

Remember "It takes a village . . . "?

Just because that village is Greenwich

Village or downtown San Francisco,

you still need to reach out and create

a community for yourself.

181

Try contacting someone who
was important in your life years ago
with whom you've lost touch. It will be
an amazing and magical moment for
both of you. We keep the past with us,
but it never springs to life with such
joy as when we reconnect with
someone we've left behind.

182

Talk to as many people as you can—the taxi driver, the cashier at the supermarket, the doorman. A life of small encounters with others brings unexpected pleasures and keeps us feeling alive and connected to the world.

183

Talk to yourself. It can be very

insightful, and it's often amusing.

And the payoff is: If you ask yourself

a question, you'll always get the

answer you're looking for.

Go toward the things that bring you a feeling of wonder. If it's animals, volunteer in a zoo; if it's a soaring building, take a class in architecture. The more we indulge our passions, the more we feel the meaning and magic in life.

Make a list of all the things
you'd love to do in the next five
years. Go wild—write all your fanta-
sies, no matter how silly they might
seem: travel to China, write a novel,
study singing, have a baby, quit your
job. Just making the list will fill you
with the joy of possibility.

186

Do you still live by the credo

that "I'll have fun when my chores

are done"? Maybe that worked in

kindergarten, but realistically, you're

not done until you're dead . . . so

you'd better start having fun today.

187

Do you ever say "Thank God
it's Monday"? If not, why not?
You spend an awful lot of time at
work; if you're not enjoying it—
maybe it's time for a change.

188

Call your mother (unless she's passed

on, or you're estranged for a really

good reason). If she's not available,

call someone else who nurtures you.

When life gets crazy-complicated, I sometimes stop and think, *What would my grandmother have done?* In most instances, she would have said, "Sit down, have a little something to eat; you'll feel better." And it works!

190

Remember that your thoughts

create your feelings and behaviors.

Positive thoughts help create

positive emotions, and may

help counter depression.

Don't underestimate the feel-good
qualities of a home-cooked meal. Invite
friends and family into your house,
as nothing makes people feel more
cared for, appreciated, and happy
than cooking and eating together.

192

Now we only see our extended families on "special occasions"—birthdays, holidays, weddings, and so on. In the old days we saw them on "ordinary" occasions, like Sunday dinners. They were always there, a constant in our lives. Wasn't it more special to have them with us more often?

When you find yourself feeling overwhelmed and you're obsessing about what you should have done or said, just use your inner voice to whack you on the head with a loud "Just stop it!" You might be able to get your own attention.

194

If you go to a department store or a restaurant and they ignore you, don't get upset; use some humor. Tell them you're a long-lost relative and that you're delighted to see them. That could get their attention, but more important, it will ease your stress.

195

On average, today's children have watched 400,000 TV commercials by the time they turn 20. Think of what the world would be like if they watched only, say, 200,000 commercials and used the rest of the time to read 1,000 books instead.

Some TV shows feed into our insecurities and put forth an inaccurate picture of what "human perfection" should be. Watching a makeover show is fun, but this kind of ideal can become ridiculous. Making yourself over until you no longer resemble yourself makes no sense!

197

People who live a little outside of

the box seem to have longer, happier

lives. Embrace your oddness.

198

Wouldn't it be great

if we all embraced each other's

differences and became one

huge global Benetton ad?

199

If you eat something that you know isn't a healthy choice, just enjoy it and be quiet. People always act as if they have to apologize: "I'll work out for two extra hours tomorrow." Who cares? Keep it between you and your stomach.

It's the people who paint outside the

lines whom we remember most vividly.

Try showing your true colors!

201

Don't get into comparative suffering, trying to outdo others in the area of work, stress, child rearing, how tired you are, and so on. Someone will always try to top you. What's the point?

202

Try to avoid eating lunch at
your desk. The mindlessness of
it makes you eat more, enjoy it less,
and resent the endless workday.
Even if the break has to be short,
take the time to think about
what you're eating, and savor it.
It will feel like a mini-vacation
in the middle of the day!

The cemetery is filled with people who no longer return their e-mails. The days of long vacations may be over, but at least turn off all your electronic devices for a few hours now and then. Take a long, deep breath and bask in the feeling that, for a short time, you're free!

If you're the boss of other people,
try to remember that fostering an
environment in which people feel
free to say what's on their minds leads to
increased productivity—and a lot more
civility. Being open to trying ideas
that are different from yours is what
makes a good manager great.

Can you dare leave the house
one day without making your bed
or doing the dishes? What will
happen? Is the voice of disapproval
in your head so strong that you can't
live with the guilt? If you're that
worried, put the dishes in the car,
and no one will find them.

Why is it that the more our country talks about exercise and fitness, the more we look like the Pillsbury Doughboy? Could it be because we really need to feed our emotions rather than our stomachs?

The physiology of human beings hasn't changed in the last 50 years, but portion sizes of food served in this country have increased by about 50 percent. Something's gotta give, and guess what it is? Our pants size! The reason "French women don't get fat" is because they eat less.

208

Why do normal people take
workshops on how to deal with
difficult people? Why aren't the
difficult people taking workshops on
how to deal with the rest of us?

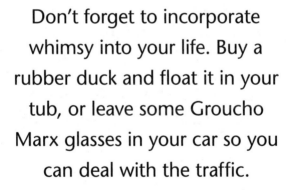

209

Don't forget to incorporate whimsy into your life. Buy a rubber duck and float it in your tub, or leave some Groucho Marx glasses in your car so you can deal with the traffic.

210

Millions of people spend weeks
and sometims months viewing celebrity
murder trials. What good can possibly
come out of doing this for days at a time?
Wouldn't we be better off watching
stories that inspire us, those revolving
around people who have accomplished
something magnificent?

Try howling once in a while.

It's a great way to feel

primal and free. And won't

the neighbors wonder,

What the heck was that?

212

We're a species that thrives on
telling stories to one another. When
you need some enlightenment in your
life, try seeking out a good story—in a
book, a movie, or in the theater. A richly
complex story about people in extraordinary
circumstances engages and refreshes
the brain as well as our souls.

Do you find yourself caring too much about the label on something— whether it's the jeans you wear or the water you drink? Maybe it would make more sense to rent yourself out as a billboard . . . then *you* could make the money instead of the person whose label you've been wearing.

Try this technique to help wean yourself from perfectionism: Force yourself to allow someone else to do something you know you can do better, and don't comment. Just live with it. How liberating! The dishwasher got stacked wrong . . . and the sun still set!

Men never seem to need to share their faults or problems the way women do. When's the last time you heard a man say that he was bloated, or that his socks were too tight? Maybe we women could learn something from this.

I love the fact that men and women are becoming more equal in many areas of life. But Rome wasn't built in a day, so continue to speak out, and become the change you want to see in others.

Men tease women for going to the bathroom in groups, but we know why we do it. The answer is very simple: Why not? Any chance to keep connected and communicate with one another is fine by us.

I'm all for open communication,
but some subjects really should be
personal. My grandmother had no idea
which of the husbands in her social circle
were good in bed and which ones weren't.
I'm not even sure their own wives knew.
Now everybody knows everything.
Sometimes a little privacy is a good thing.

Stand up and give your seat to the elderly. Not only is it good karma ('cause you'll want that seat someday), but it also simply makes the world a better place, and you a more decent part of it.

220

Accept the things you cannot

change, change the things you can,

and laugh at the rest.

221

The one constant in

life is that things happen,

and usually when you're

not in the mood for them.

You know the old saying about how we all see a cup as half full or half empty? Well, I say both options stink. I want my cup running over! If you see your life as a cup that's always full of the wonders of life, your days will be full to bursting.

If you're a parent, remember, you're the boss. You don't have to give your children a reason for everything you're doing. Sometimes *you* just need to make the decisions. Why? Because you're the parent.

An average five-year-old child laughs

more than four hundred times a day.

An adult? Fourteen. Do you think that's

why so many adults need laxatives?

225

Laptop computers are for

working while you're traveling.

They're not for checking e-mail

during dinner at Aunt Emily's.

Some people save all their "good"' things for a special occasion. No sitting on the good furniture; no eating off the good dishes; certainly don't drink from the wedding crystal. Which occasion do you think they're waiting for? Their funeral, when only other people will enjoy the good stuff?

227

Have you ever thought of calling in "well"? We all have sick days, but more important, wouldn't it be great to honor our health instead of speak to our illnesses.

228

Smile more often. Scientists now believe that the simple act of smiling, even if you have nothing in particular to smile about, will in fact improve your mood. Smile during sex and God knows what might happen!

A sense of humor gives us the ability

to shift perspective and be flexible.

And flexibility is the ability to not

get bent out of shape.

230

For years I heard my mother's
stern voice in my head whenever I
cleaned the house: "Make sure you
scrub the underside of the toilet bowl!"
I finally realized that no one that short
was ever coming to visit, and I didn't
give a damn. What voices do you
carry in *your* head?

Try writing down the things
you actually did on a particular day:
called Mom, cooked dinner, bought
a birthday present for Erica, paid the
phone bill. At the end of the day,
celebrate your "done list" instead of
dreading your "to-do" list.

We've been brainwashed
into thinking that shopping is
a leisure activity. Our grandparents
bought what they needed with a frugal
eye and saved their money. Sometimes
learning to say no to our desires is the
best way to improve our lives.

Every child needs structure and discipline, but just be careful not to act like you're running a boot camp. Your kids need to see that you, too, can be a kid once in a while. The family that laughs together . . . stays together.

234

Whenever there's something
that you fear you can't accomplish,
can you think of *The Little Engine That
Could?* There's a great deal of wisdom
in that story. And sometimes it takes
a child's viewpoint to get some
hard things done.

If your life is beginning to
feel like a runaway train, grab
ahold of the emergency cord and
jump off. You just might be on
a fast track to nowhere.

Pavlov showed us that we
animals can continually behave in
a certain way when we're conditioned
to do so. Repeating the same behavior
over and over might be okay for a lab
rat, but it's not much fun for human
beings . . . unless your ultimate goal
is to get a piece of cheese.

237

Depression isn't something to live
with or try to get over on your own.
Reach out and get help. You should
never live your life as if you're wearing
a black shroud standing under a black
cloud. You deserve much more.

Try to be consistent in setting limits with your children. Being erratic with discipline will soon have your child thinking, *Maybe I didn't get away with it this time, but trust me, I'll keep trying.*

Be clear what you expect from your children. Saying things like "You never listen to me" or "You never help me" just serves to reinforce what they're already doing.

When you feel taken advantage
of at home or at work, don't sulk
and say things like "Nobody cares."
Why tell them the obvious? They
don't care. Clearly let them know
what you really *do* want . . . it
might just get you some respect.

241

When you set a goal for
yourself, make it realistic.
Saying that you're going to lose
20 pounds in one week is like
asking a mouse to chase a cat.
It isn't going to happen.

242

There's so much grace in acceptance.

It's not an easy concept, but if you

embrace it, you'll find more peace

than you ever imagined.

243

Happiness isn't a task to be

fulfilled. It's there in the precious,

everyday moments. If you seek it too

hard, you'll miss it.

244

I love to hear someone say they have options. It illustrates a mind that sees life like a Ben & Jerry's ice-cream parlor: lots of flavors with great fixings to mix in.

245

Invest some time and energy
being with all types of people of
every color and size. Steep yourself
in diversity. It will open up your
world and make you more
of a global citizen.

Lose the black-and-white thinking.
Nothing is always the same, even if you
think it is. Life ebbs and flows, and even
if you believe that it "always" rains on
your day off, or that you can "never"
find a parking spot, it doesn't make
it so. You just want to be right.

247

Life is not a stress rehearsal.

So why practice making daily life

a drama when you could create a

musical or a comedy?

248

"The best is yet to come" is a great

phrase to live by, but the best might

also be here, right now. If you live for

later, you might totally miss *now*.

Lighten up! Life is too short

to take too seriously.

250

If you're driving someplace

with a man, remember that he

doesn't like to ask for directions.

That's why Moses was in the

desert for 40 years.

Women are incredibly adept at a martial art called "tongue fu." So when you decide to engage in an argument with a female, keep in mind that you're no match for someone who can take you down with loquacious license.

Be aware that your mind contains
enough material to keep you amused
all day. It's like an inner sitcom that
can entertain you for days on end,
without any commercial breaks!

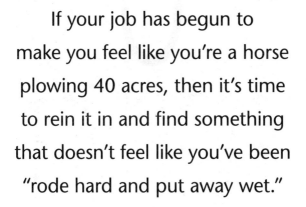

253

If your job has begun to make you feel like you're a horse plowing 40 acres, then it's time to rein it in and find something that doesn't feel like you've been "rode hard and put away wet."

254

Keep a journal of your life.

It will be a great gift for those who

follow, and it will help you discover

whether your history has helped

or hindered you (or them).

255

Don't answer the phone during dinner. It will only serve to remove you from fully enjoying one of the most pleasurable experiences of life. And no one needs you that desperately unless you're an emergency-room physician.

When you have a day off, don't spend it trying to do everything you didn't do the rest of the week. It will only make you feel overwhelmed and undernurtured. Instead, reflect on how to manage your time; otherwise, you're left with no time for you.

257

Don't become obsessive about

anything! It will only make you

feel like a dart that's always trying

to hit the bull's-eye.

There's nothing like chocolate.

Keep some next to your bed.

It's simply orgasmic.

259

When it rains,
really listen. It's like a
meditation accompanied
by drops of water.

260

Not getting what you want may

just be a grand stroke of luck.

261

When you depart this earth, may you

leave it knowing that you were well

used and that all who knew you felt

blessed by your presence.

262

Life is like a buffet. Indulge in every-

thing it has to offer, and sample little

tastes of all that's wonderful.

We spend a lot more time exercising our bodies than we do exercising our brains. What good are tight abs if we have a flabby brain? Keep your mind pumped by learning new things, doing puzzles, reading, or mastering a new language. It's sweat free, and you don't have to take a shower afterward.

Some of us don't like to talk about politics for fear of alienating others—but if you hide your true beliefs, then you might keep a friend while losing yourself. Don't live on a soapbox, but do stand up for what you believe.

Can you remember times when you were particularly tender with other people in your life—or even with yourself? A time when you really connected with true empathy and affection? Try to bask in that feeling often.

Don't wait for a holiday

or a birthday to have a party.

Why not plan a menopause,

divorce, or great-hair-day party . . .

or just have one for the heck of it.

267

If you can't get to sleep, don't
toss and turn and wonder why you
can't. The more you try to figure it
out, the less likely you are to actually
fall asleep. Get up and do something
to distract yourself. You'll soon
feel yourself getting drowsy.

268

Clothing can change your mood.

Try a splash of color; wear funky

glasses; or a big, bold hat. It can turn

a dreary day into one filled with fun.

269

Stop watching reruns of *Friends* and start bonding with some real friends! So many of us allow TV and other media to take the place of real human connections. Tune out and tune in . . . to some real people.

270

Who in your life drives you crazy?

Do they elicit negative feelings

in you? Cut to the chase:

Spend less time or let them go!

271

We all tend to talk too much about our problems. Transform your thoughts and conversations into solutions, and you'll find that some of your stress will melt away.

By nature, we all tend to want to acquire more and bigger things, but what are the things that *really* make life wonderful? Can you try to truly honor and appreciate the simple joys? Is it the giggle of a child in your life? The smell of cookies baking? The sounds of an afternoon near the sea?

Try volunteering your time to clean up a park, to be a school crossing guard, to help the elderly get a hot meal, or even just say hello to neighbors. You'll feel the rush of energy and importance that comes along with being connected and contributing to a part of a bigger world.

The next time there's a setback,

instead of thinking, *Nothing ever goes*

my way, how about considering how

much *has* gone your way!

Try to find inspiration in wondrous creations of the human spirit, such as Beethoven's Ninth Symphony, the *Mona Lisa*, the Chrysler Building, or the classic movie *It's a Wonderful Life*. You'll have your own selection, but you'll find that it's hard to obsess over minutiae when you feel inspired by greatness.

Don't promise things you can't deliver. We're all way too busy to do everything we have to do—but telling somebody that you'll have a task done on Tuesday when you probably can't get it done before the weekend simply makes everyone feel bad. You feel overstressed, and the other person feels cheated.

Try counting your blessings
instead of counting the things you
don't have, especially before you go
to bed. When you put yourself to
sleep with thoughts of the wonders
in your life, you honor the world
and the people around you.

Get plenty of sleep. Our bodies need rest, and our brains need the escape of dreams. Those of us who would never think of abusing our bodies with, say, drugs, think nothing of abusing our bodies' need for rejuvenation and rest. For God's sake, take a nap!

Pessimists may be more

accurate, but optimists

live longer.

Try to think of something you appreciate
when you're getting anxious. Anxiety is
based in fear; appreciation is bathed in
love. The more appreciative you are, the
more your fears will go down the drain.

We tend to spend a lot of time
and excess energy wishing that
our lives were different. Why give
up all that time to a fairy tale?

Prayer can be a powerful tool for inner peace. Even for those of us who aren't religious, the use of a mantra, or even a meaningful poem, can give us a path to natural inner solitude and bring us more in touch with our higher selves.

283

Stop making excuses for the things

you aren't doing. No one wants

to hear you tell them what you're

going to do day in and day out.

Either do it . . . or don't!

Be dramatic! Be flamboyant!
How much more fun is it to
emulate or become an individual
who has style and panache?
It's much better than looking
like part of the wallpaper.

285

If you find it hard to say no,

just say, "I'll think about it and

get back to you later."

Buy yourself a whip. Why not?
You beat yourself up anyway over
small things, right? Why not go all the
way and really self-flagellate? And just
maybe, when you reach for the whip,
you'll realize how ridiculous it is to be
beating up on yourself, and you can
celebrate the moment instead.

Give yourself an award today, or

ask for a standing ovation. Even if

it's just for preparing a fabulous

breakfast, getting the kids to school

on time, or just breathing—

we all need acknowledgment.

288

Indulge in pleasure whenever you

can. Eat dessert first, take a bath in

the middle of the day, or watch a

squirrel fall off a bird feeder.

The first time I heard the phrase "anti-aging formula," I thought, *What's that? Hemlock?* Anything that's anti-aging has to kill you, because if you're alive, you're aging. Learn to accept and enjoy the preciousness of life and the fun you can have at any age.

290

Create a family mission
statement. What are your
values? What do you enjoy?
What do you want to change?
Think about it.

Do some of your behaviors make you feel like a gerbil on a wheel? Things that you just do over and over that never get you anywhere—but that leave you exhausted anyway? Is there a way to get off the wheel? Or like a gerbil, would you prefer to just nibble on a carrot and then get right back to it?

Write your own eulogy. It's a powerful exercise to imagine what you want said at your funeral. And, if you can be completely honest with yourself during this exercise, maybe it will help illuminate a path to change some aspects of your life before the real thing happens.

When you find yourself saying things that make no sense just because you're stressed out by traffic or a fax machine jamming, try really listening to yourself, and then answer yourself back. For instance, "Where did all these cars come from? Oh, I get it—it's a road!"

Remember when your mother told you to get going and stop acting like you're in la-la land? Well, go back there every once in a while. It will give you a respite from your adult world.

295

Never stop asking yourself

what you want to be when

you grow up.

Avoid euphemisms such as "downsizing," "weight challenged," and "intellectually impaired." These phrases don't kid anybody. You got fired, you gained weight, and maybe you just don't get it.

Try to exaggerate your
minor irritations. It might give
you some distance to put things
into perspective. When your computer
crashes, tell everyone about it and
then just twirl. You'll find yourself
cracking up instead of falling apart.

Say "Thank you" often.

It may be the greatest prayer

you'll ever utter.

If tomorrow were your last day

alive, what would you like

people to remember about you?

Be a mentor to someone.
You'll not only discover how much
you know and see how valuable
your experience is—you'll feel
great for passing it on and helping
someone get on their way.

301

Surround yourself with old magazines, and start cutting and pasting. Make a collage that illustrates the life you have now, and one that illustrates the life you want. The contrasts will astound you, and perhaps show you an interesting new path.

Can you give up on your need to be

right all the time? It's hard to have

fun if you're always proving a point.

Someone who thinks
that there's a "silver lining" in
every cloud is a Pollyanna. And
Pollyannas are passive and
ineffective. Try optimism—it's
effective and life enhancing.

304

Try looking into someone's eyes when you're talking to them. The connection is amazing. It's the gateway to the soul.

305

Think about what you're

thinking about. And don't

believe everything you think.

Exercise can help you

with bad moods. It changes

your focus and helps your

mind and your heart.

Try to allow your children some free time. We all hate the fact that our lives are so busy and over-scheduled, and then what do we do? Schedule three after-school activities every day for our kids, and then leave no time for them to just hang around and be silly with their friends! Six-year-olds shouldn't need a day planner to keep their lives in order.

308

Don't follow someone else's

dictates to the point of leaving

your own perspective. That's

called a cult. Think for yourself—

that's called intelligence.

Don't allow yourself to be fooled by ad agencies that use clever packaging to appeal to modern sensibilities. A peanut butter-and-chocolate Power Bar is still just a big chunk of candy.

310

Learn to love waiting. We'd all
love to be in the front of the line, but
let's face it, it's not always possible.
When you're waiting, you have the
opportunity to relax, and to smile at
someone else who's waiting.

If nothing makes sense to you,

you just might be in a place

where you haven't used enough

of your common sense.

312

You must face the past,

and then get past it so you

can live in the present.

Realize that you can be your

own entertainment center. If you

show up, you can pretty much

guarantee that you'll have fun.

You have to realize that a
healthy relationship comes from
understanding how to relate. If you
spend a lot of time communicating how
needy you are, all you can expect to
find is someone who's just as needy.

315

Every day, try to have as much
fun as possible. That will enable
you to better deal with any crisis that
you come up against. The more you
give yourself the experience of
happiness, the more it truly fortifies
you to deal with unhappiness.

316

Every time you take a walk,

realize that you have incredible

powers to move forward. When you

sit around, you simply magnify

your ability to stay stuck.

Make and keep good friends;

they give you the opportunity to

be yourself. Relatives are great,

but they may never understand

you the way your friends do.

Grandchildren are the kids we should have had first. And unless we're truly deluded, we can be pretty sure we won't repeat the same mistakes.

Our parents did the best they could with the information they had at the time they raised us. If we could all acknowledge this, we would spend less time making judgments and more time being compassionate.

You don't have to spend a lifetime wishing you hadn't done this or that. Skip to what you can and could do now; it's much more invigorating and much less depressing.

321

Our ideal partner should be someone who shares our values, lives with
passion, and encourages us to do the
same. "Opposites might attract," but
they could also be a lot of work.

322

Don't make everything your fault.

Instead, praise yourself for all the

good things you do. That's it . . .

pat yourself on the back!

Don't watch the news broadcasts
every day. Most of what you hear
will be frightening and stressful. Don't
worry about being out of touch—
there's always someone around
who loves to spread bad news, and
you'll find out soon enough.

Try to listen to upbeat music. The melody and lyrics will help your mind and body feel happy and content. Frantic sounds with dark words only make you feel like you're going to hell in a handbasket.

325

Whenever you're waiting in
line, connect with as many people
around you as possible. You may
make new friends, you might find
yourself laughing with someone,
and the time you felt was wasted
will become time well spent.

326

No one respects a martyr unless they're giving their life to save another. Believing that people are going to canonize you because you cleaned the house or spent extra hours at work is not the pathway to sainthood. I have yet to see a statue called "Sister of Perpetual Responsibility."

327

If you love someone more
than you love yourself, then you can
almost guarantee that this person
now has a slave. Just remember that
the slaves were freed; you might
want to do the same for yourself.

Listen to the wind whenever you

can. It often whispers words of

wisdom that you can't hear in

the chaos of everyday life.

We spend so much time judging ourselves and others. What would happen if we allowed ourselves to just accept the fact that none of us is perfect?

330

Don't allow yourself to get caught up in believing that being rail thin is a worthy goal in life. The models and celebrities who look that way make it their life's work: They have trainers, cooks, and housekeepers at their bidding. But all of that aside, looking like a broom with legs isn't that appealing.

Remember that not everyone

thrives in an organized space.

You may just flourish in chaos.

Don't you think you have enough
hair products? You might want to keep
only one or two and put the cash you
save into a money-market account so
that when you get older you'll be able
to afford your own hairdresser.

333

Did you ever look into a cat's eyes?

They seem both amused and wise.

I can hear them thinking . . . *You know*

what I know; you just aren't ready.

You may want to go to a mall and
just watch people as they pass by.
Do the ones with the bags full of
stuff look any happier than the ones
with no bags? If not, then perhaps
the question to ask ourselves is:
*Does having a lot of stuff
really make us happy?*

335

When you look at a child's face,

it is absent of frowns and wrinkles.

Is it simply because their youth keeps

the lines at bay? Or is the ability to

be present, laugh a lot, and have

fun the *real* wrinkle cream?

When you read all the latest
and greatest articles on how to
reduce stress, doesn't it make
you feel even more stressed out?

When you talk to your children, make sure that you don't give them more messages about growing up than you do about enjoying their childhood. In fact, you may want to grab on to some of their spirit. It could help you grow younger while you're growing older.

When you get yourself all upset

over everyday minutiae, imagine

yourself doing it wearing a big clown

nose. It's pretty hard to stay upset

when your life becomes a circus act.

Have you ever danced naked?
If not, why not? Try it alone or
with your beloved. If he or she
doesn't like it, you may want to
reconsider who you're with. If
you don't like it, you might want
to reconsider who *you* are.

Try to shout "Whoopee!" or "Whee!"

as you walk down the street or drive

your car. It sets off a cascade of

feelings that speak to being fully alive.

The *eeeeee*s at the end of the

words are like sonic caffeine.

341

If you consider failure to be a
lesson for success, then you just
might have more knowledge
than you ever dreamed of.

342

Make sure that you belt out

a song that you love every once

in a while. There's nothing better

than hearing your voice doing

something other than the same

old blah, blah, blah.

343

If you get to your wit's end,

you may just be a nitwit.

Have you ever looked up at the sky and become overwhelmed by its vastness? It's a great thing to do, because it allows you to realize that you're simply a small piece of something much greater than the world you know.

Whenever you're eating something you love, make sure you moan with delight. It enhances the flavors and allows your body to feel like a king at a feast. Just remember to make your feasting diminutive versus colossal. Otherwise you may end up looking like Henry VIII.

Don't you just love your bed? It embraces you and allows you to stretch, roll over, and rest with delight. Treat yourself to a good mattress; it will give you much sweeter dreams than a lumpy one, which could foster nightmares.

347

Give your brain some exercise with
a few new simple ideas. Brush your teeth
with the opposite hand, towel yourself
dry differently, and take a different street
to work. It's a wonderful way to give
your brain some new routing.

348

No amount of moaning and groaning changes a rainy day to one that radiates with sun. You just have to decide to enjoy the rain and be your own sunshine.

Being afraid of everything is

incredibly debilitating. Anything

can happen at any time, whether

you fear it or not. So why bother?

350

Don't wait for special

occasions to celebrate.

Every day is a special occasion.

351

If anyone ever says to you,

"Oh, you're just too much,"

thank them and say, "There's

a whole lot more where

that came from. . . ."

352

If you have a cold or the flu, stay home and take care of yourself. You don't need to share it with your co-workers. That's called selfish.

Whenever you start to catastrophize about something, can you see that you're becoming the finale of your own Shakespearean play? If you want to play Hamlet or King Lear, then you should audition for the part and get paid. Otherwise, it's just a waste of time.

354

Write a letter of gratitude
to someone you feel has made
a real difference in your life.
Then read it to this individual
in person. Both of you will
benefit in body, mind, and
spirit for years to come.

Choose some movies every once in a while that reflect your own life. Who knows what a little cinema therapy can do for your psyche? It may help you find solutions, or it could just make you see that you're not alone in how you feel.

If you want to keep a man

attracted to you, don't become

his mother. He already had one

of those, and one is enough.

Buy some big, fat, fluffy slippers

to wear at the end of the day.

They'll help make your feet feel

cozy, and happy feet will take you

wherever you want to go.

Have you ever wondered

what a Miracle Bra is really all about?

Well, when you take it off and

exclaim "Free at last!" . . . that's

when the miracle begins.

359

Make sure you choose comfort-

able clothing. Life is difficult enough

without spending the day feeling like

your clothes are out to kill you.

360

When you're driving your car,

instead of getting upset about traffic,

play a language tape or an audio book

and spend the time learning. Your

car can be a university on wheels

instead of a hell on wheels.

361

Don't forget the power of touch. Our skin covers

our entire body. Make sure you or someone

else explores as much territory as possible. We,

as a culture, suffer from skin hunger, so feed

your skin just as much as you feed your tummy.

362

Spend some time in awe of your body. Speak to it with kindness, compassion, and empathy. It's done a lot for you, despite what you've done to it, good or bad.

363

Random acts of kindness are okay,

but living and behaving kindly

every day really makes sense.

364

It's okay to delegate responsibilities

to others. Then you can have time off

from having to tell everyone you have

to do everything yourself.

365

And above all else,

remember that feeling good . . .

feels good!

About the Author

Loretta LaRoche is an internationally renowned author and stress-management consultant who advocates humor, optimism, and resiliency as coping mechanisms. She uses her wit and wisdom to help people learn how to take stress and turn it into strengths, and how to see themselves as the survivors of their own lives—that is, to find the "bless in the mess." Loretta is a favorite with viewers of her six PBS specials, as well as on the lecture circuit, where she presents an average of 100 talks per year. She lives in Plymouth, Massachusetts.

Website: **www.lorettalaroche.com**

Notes

Notes

Hay House Titles of Related Interest

Everyday Positive Thinking
by Louise L. Hay and Friends

Everyday Wisdom
by Dr. Wayne W. Dyer

Everything I've Ever Done That Worked
by Lesley Garner

The Gift of Peace
by Ben Stein

Never Mind Success . . . Go for Greatness!
by Tavis Smiley

101 Ways to Jump-Start Your Intuition
by John Holland

⸺◈◈◈⸺

All of the above are available at your local bookstore,
or may be ordered by contacting:
Hay House (see next page).

⸺◈◈◈⸺

We hope you enjoyed this Hay House Lifestyles book.
If you'd like to receive a free catalog featuring additional
Hay House books and products, or if you'd like information
about the Hay Foundation, please contact:

Hay House, Inc.
P.O. Box 5100
Carlsbad, CA 92018-5100

(760) 431-7695 or **(800) 654-5126**
(760) 431-6948 (fax) or **(800) 650-5115 (fax)**
www.hayhouse.com® • **www.hayfoundation.org**

Published and distributed in Australia by:
Hay House Australia Pty. Ltd. • 18/36 Ralph St. • Alexandria NSW
2015 • *Phone:* 612-9669-4299 • *Fax:* 612-9669-4144 •
www.hayhouse.com.au

Published and distributed in the United Kingdom by:
Hay House UK, Ltd. • Unit 62, Canalot Studios • 292 Kensal
Rd., London W10 5BE • *Phone:* 44-20-8962-1230 •
Fax: 44-20-8962-1239 • www.hayhouse.co.uk

Published and distributed in the Republic of South Africa by:
Hay House SA (Pty), Ltd., P.O. Box 990, Witkoppen 2068 •
Phone/Fax: 27-11-706-6612 • orders@psdprom.co.za

Published in India by:
Hay House Publications (India) Pvt. Ltd., 3 Hampton
Court, A-Wing, 123 Wodehouse Rd., Colaba, Mumbai
400005 • *Phone:* 91 (22) 22150557 or 22180533 •
Fax: 91 (22) 22839619 • www.hayhouseindia.co.in

Distributed in India by:
Media Star, 7 Vaswani Mansion, 120 Dinshaw
Vachha Rd., Churchgate, Mumbai 400020 • *Phone:*
91 (22) 22815538-39-40 • *Fax:* 91 (22) 22839619 •
booksdivision@mediastar.co.in

Distributed in Canada by:
Raincoast • 9050 Shaughnessy St., Vancouver, B.C.
V6P 6E5 • *Phone:* (604) 323-7100 • *Fax:* (604) 323-2600 •
www.raincoast.com

Tune in to **HayHouseRadio.com**™ for the best in
inspirational talk radio featuring top Hay House authors!
And, sign up via the Hay House USA Website to receive the
Hay House online newsletter and stay informed about what's
going on with your favorite authors. You'll receive bimonthly
announcements about: Discounts and Offers, Special Events,
Product Highlights, Free Excerpts, Giveaways, and more!
www.hayhouse.com®